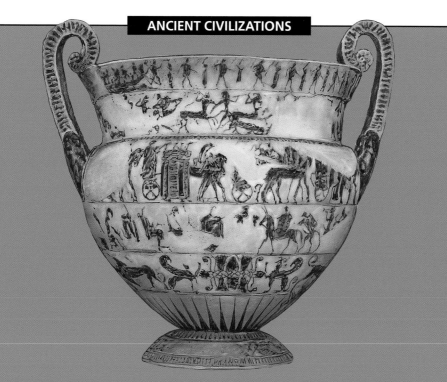

GREECE

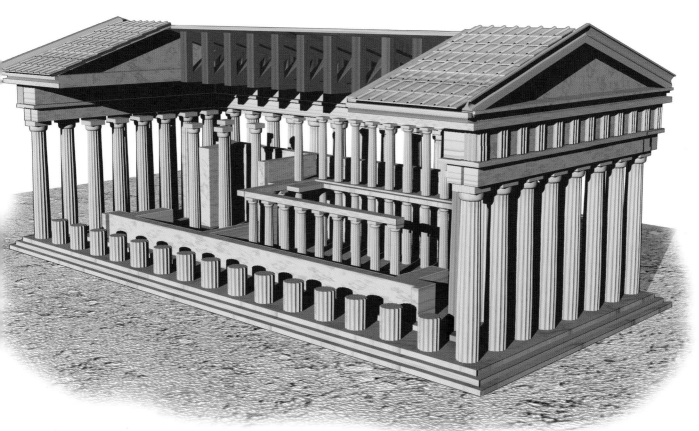

CHELSEA HOUSE
PUBLISHERS
A Haights Cross Communications Company ®

First hardcover library edition published
in the United States of America in
2006 by Chelsea House Publishers,
a subsidiary of Haights Cross Communications.
All rights reserved.

A Haights Cross Communications ✈ Company ®

www.chelseahouse.com

Library of Congress Cataloging-in-Publication Data

Bargalló i Chaves, Eva, 1960-
[Grecia. English]
Greece / Eva Bargalló.
    p. cm. — (Ancient civilizations)
ISBN 0-7910-8605-4 (hardcover)
1. Greece—Civilization—To 146 B.C.—Juvenile
literature. I. Title. II. Ancient civilizations
(Philadelphia, Pa.).
DF77.B264 2005
938--dc22   2004027161

Project and realization
Parramón Ediciones, S.A.

Texts
Eva Bargalló

Translator
Patrick Clark

Graphic Design and Typesetting
Estudi Toni Inglés (Alba Marco)

Illustrations
Marcel Socías Studio

First edition – February 2004

Printed in Spain
© Parramón Ediciones, S.A. – 2004
Ronda de Sant Pere, 5, 4ª planta
08010 Barcelona (España)
Empresa del Grupo Editorial Norma

www.parramon.com

ON THE SHORES OF THE MEDITERRANEAN

Nearly three thousand years ago, in an extensive region bathed by the waters of the Mediterranean Sea, one of most influential and long-lasting civilizations in human history, the Greek civilization, developed. This culture was outstanding not only for the beauty and mastery of its artistic and architectural masterpieces, but also for its wisdom, scientific knowledge, and elevated level of political and social development.

For all of these reasons, we want to introduce young readers to the main features of this passionate civilization. We begin this work with a brief introduction in the form of a summary and a temporal framework for the eleven topics that will be developed in the rest of the book. These topics are guided by a short opening narrative and organized according to a central illustration that serves to explain, in a clear and concise way, different aspects of Greek culture and history as they relate to the illustration. Additional drawings also expand on the content or offer additional information.

To make reading easier and complement the information contained in the text, the last two pages of the book include a glossary of terms and a chronology, in which the main political and cultural events of Greek history are outlined.

In the selection of topics and the development of the content, attractiveness took precedence over exhaustiveness. Our primary objectives are to awaken in the young reader an interest in the history of great civilizations, without overwhelming him or her with excessive historical data, and at the same time, to encourage the student to embark on further study of this material.

THE ORIGINS OF WESTERN CIVILIZATION

The palaces of Crete were decorated with fresco paintings, as in this detail from a work dated between 1400 B.C. and 1380 B.C.

THE CRETAN OR MINOAN CIVILIZATION

More than four thousand years ago, people of Indo-European origins, conditioned by their geographical surroundings, began to navigate and develop one of the most brilliant and surprising cultures of the Mediterranean: the Cretan or Minoan culture. The inhabitants of Crete, an island bathed by the waters of the sea that had witnessed so many civilizations, built great palaces based around patio structures, richly decorated with paintings of female dancers and acrobats, as well as still lifes and very natural-looking animals. These enormous buildings with their labyrinths not only sheltered the royal family, but also housed officials, artisans, and servants.

Archaeological excavations allow us to date these palaces and to record the existence of two stages: the first stage, which lasted approximately until 1700 B.C., would end with the destruction of the palaces, in all likelihood due to a natural disaster; the second period, characterized by the rebuilding of the royal residences, probably disappeared as a result of Mycenaean expansion.

THE MYCENAEANS: A COMBATIVE AND EXPANSIONIST PEOPLE

Remains in Greece show evidence of a warrior-like civilization. This society that was able to build large fortresses and protected palaces, dates back to about 1600 B.C. Some architectural elements of these remains allow us to compare this culture to Minoan culture, although it seems that such defensive structures did not exist in that society. Investigations done in Mycenae, the most important of the cities, and the place that gives the name to this civilization, uncovered royal tombs with a circular floor plan and a cover similar to a vaulted ceiling. Inside objects and jewels were made of precious metals, such as the gold mask attributed to Agamemnon.

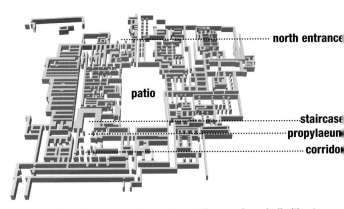

north entrance

patio

staircase
propylaeum
corridor

A sketch of the floor plan of the palace at Knossos has similarities to a labyrinth, in that the different rooms are organized around a central patio.

Woman of Auxerre. The simplicity of forms, the hieratic style, the lack of movement, and the forward-facing direction of this figure correspond to the characteristics of ancient sculptures.

A LONG PERIOD OF MORE THAN FOUR HUNDRED YEARS

The Achaian people who settled on mainland Greece and Crete were invaded by another warrior tribe, the Dorians, who destroyed Mycenae. The Achaians, who had assimilated Minoan culture, were forced to scatter to the islands of the Aegean Sea and the coasts of Asia Minor.

More than four centuries passed before a new civilization arose. Little is known about this long period called the Dark Age or the Greek Middle Age. Archaeological excavations allow us to conclude that the invasions at the end of the thirteenth century B.C. were accompanied by the abandonment and the destruction of most Mycenaen locations, not necessarily followed by new settlements by the invading peoples.

Gradually, the mix of populations created a flourishing culture that offered its first contributions starting in the eighth century B.C.

THE EFFERVESCENCE OF THE HELLENIC WORLD

Between the eighth and the sixth centuries B.C., the basis was established for a culture that revolutionized not only the fields of art and literature but also abstract thought, the sciences, and politics. This period, called Archaic, gave way to a period of even greater flourishing, the Classical epoch, which in turn, gave way to the Hellenic period. This period represents the culmination and the later decadence of a civilization that, even today, represents an important part of Western cultural heritage.

The lions' door of Mycenae is constructed with huge blocks. In a block of stone resting on the threshold, two lions appear, separated by a central column.

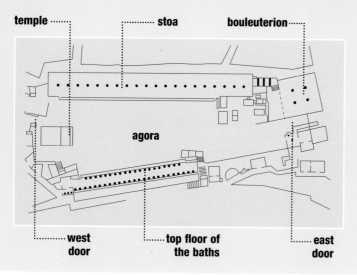

temple ..... stoa ..... bouleuterion .....

agora

west door ..... top floor of the baths ..... east door

Floor plan of the agora in Assos. Around the plaza, a meeting place for citizens, the most important civic buildings of the polis, such as the bouleuterion and the stoa, were built.

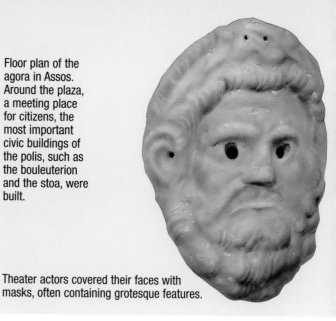

Theater actors covered their faces with masks, often containing grotesque features.

Throughout those centuries, the Greeks, whose economy was based on agriculture, cattle raising, and commerce, expanded across the Mediterranean and founded colonies in places as distant as Ampurias, Odessa, and Neukratis. At the same time, they fought long and cruel wars among themselves or with other cultures, such as the Persians. Figures such as Pericles and Alexander the Great brought glory to their country. Alexander the Great also extended the frontiers of the Hellenic world beyond what his predecessors had dreamed possible, forming an immense empire that, unfortunately, lasted only a short time. Upon his death, the empire was divided between his more ambitious generals. This division was the main cause of the decline of Hellenistic civilization.

HUMAN BEINGS, THE AXIS OF SOCIETY

Human beings are the main point of interest in this new Mediterranean civilization. They are the center of the universe, and their minds become the object of study. The sciences, literature, art, architecture, and religion all focus around humanity, and their starting point is the thoughts, passions, needs, and bodies of human beings.

In philosophy, an attempt was made to define the nature of the world; from these beginnings, disciplines such as mathematics, astronomy, and the sciences were developed. Afterward, based on their understanding of the nature of human beings, the Greeks began to try to find proper norms for individual and social behavior.

Religion played a very important role in the daily lives of the Greeks, because every city was under the patronage of a god and many festivities were celebrated in the local god's honor. In addition, there were more general events, such as the Olympic Games in honor of Zeus or the Dionysiac festivals in honor of the god of wine and fertility. The gods took human form, and the mythological tales of their relationships and adventures reflect the passion and suffering of human beings.

With regard to political organization, the idea of the *polis*, an independent city-state that dominated the people of the surrounding area, was developed. Sometimes, several city-states formed alliances to defend themselves from external dangers, such as happened during the Persian Wars; or, they fought with each

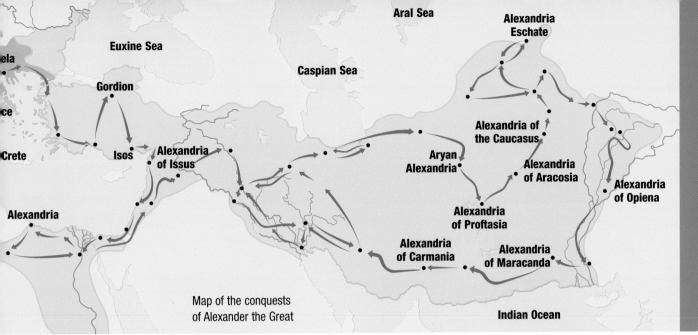

Map of the conquests
of Alexander the Great

other, as did Athens and Sparta on repeated occasions. The most important political institutions over the course of Greek history were the monarchy (government by a single person), the oligarchy (government by a few), the aristocracy (government by the nobility), and the democracy (government of the people).

In the world of Greek architecture and the arts in general, the artist ceases to be anonymous and is recognized for his achievements. Building, sculpture, and painting claim to embody harmony, equilibrium, and proportion, with human beings being the measure of all things. The human figure goes from being crudely represented to reaching elevated levels of perfection of movement and proportion. Greek citizens showed a passion for the theater. The festivals of Dionysus evolved into tragedy, splendidly represented by Aeschylus, Sophocles, and Euripides, and into comedy, of which Aristophanes was the leading playwright.

THE BIRTH OF A STAR AND THE DECLINE OF A GREAT CIVILIZATION

The conquests of the military genius Alexander the Great in the fourth century B.C. opened the doors of the Hellenic world to influences and cultures from the East. Art became more expressive and colossal, and artistic forms evolved toward a more baroque style; contacts with other schools of thought and with the rich cities of the East formed the basis for scientific advances, crowned with notable discoveries, and the development of philosophy, with diversification into distinct schools of thought.

However, the imperial dream of the Macedonian conqueror was cut off by his premature death. His vast dominions were divided between his generals, thus setting off a long period of decline that culminated with the incorporation of Greece into the great Roman Empire.

Asclepius, god of medicine. He is usually depicted as a pensive man holding onto a stick, with a serpent coiled around it.

THE FABULOUS ANCIENT GREECE

In the eighth century B.C., Dorian, Ionian, and Aeolian civilizations invaded Greek lands and forced the original inhabitants to withdraw to the coasts of present-day Turkey and the Aegean Islands, putting an end to the brilliant Mycenaean culture. A few centuries later, these lands, whose coasts are washed by the Mediterranean Sea, saw the growth of ancient Greece, one of the greatest Western civilizations.

Delphi ■
in this city the most prestigious of the ancient oracles was located, that of Apollo; the remains of his sanctuary survive here to this day

Italian peninsula

Olympus ■
religious and cultural center of ancient Greece; every four years, it was transformed into the capital of sports with the celebration of the pan-Hellenic Olympic Games

Sparta ■
after Athens, the most important city-state of ancient Greece; it maintained a very rigid and notably warlike social structure

Mediterranean Sea

Crete ■
one of the most extraordinary pre-Hellenic civilizations developed on this island: the Cretan or Minoan culture

■ Mycenae

the most powerful city on mainland Greece between 1600 B.C. and 1200 B.C. Archaeological excavations have uncovered many remains corresponding to Mycenaean culture

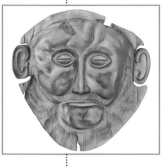

ALPHA AND BETA

Did you know that the word "alphabet" was formed from the first two letters of the ancient Greek alphabet? The Greeks invented a new alphabet, based on the Phoenician alphabet, which allowed the development of literature, and was one of the seeds for the extraordinary growth of Greek thought and culture.

■ Troy

city that was the setting for the Trojan War, which was immortalized by Homer in the *Iliad*

■ Ionia

region on the central part of the west coast of Asia Minor, inhabited by the Ionians; outstanding cities such as Miletus and Ephesus flourished here

Macedonia

Black Sea

unt Olympus

Aegean Sea

Anatolia

Ephesus

Miletus

Peloponnese

■ Thebes

the most important city in the region of Boeotia where excellent paintings from the Mycenaean era remain

■ Athens

the most important and influential city-state of ancient Greece, as much from the political point of view as artistically and culturally

Africa

A WELL OF WISDOM

In the Greek city-states there was an open area, call the agora, where, in addition to gathering in assemblies and going to the market, citizens met to discuss subjects of interest to the community. This shared public space favored the development of disciplines such as philosophy, mathematics, history, and medicine, to the point of founding distinct schools and branches whose achievements have created the basis for Western thought and science.

THE PEOPLE'S GOVERNMENT

Democracy was born in Greece, thanks most of all to three men: Dracon, who put together the first written code of laws in Athens; Solon, who produced a new constitution; and Cleisthenes, who carried out the democratic reform of the Athenian constitution.

Aristotle ■
the thinking of this great Greek philosopher and scientist, a disciple of Plato, has been influential and enduring throughout history; he also founded a school, the Lyceum, where he put together a large library

Hippocrates ■
considered the father of medicine because he established the basis of medical science and established the natural character of all diseases; he was also one of the first scientists to separate science from religion

■ **Herodotus**
this historian made many voyages to collect information for his famous *Histories*

Pythagoras ■
Greek philosopher and mathematician, founder of the school of thought and the theory that bear his name

■ **agora**
the central square of the polis, around which the main civic buildings of the city were built

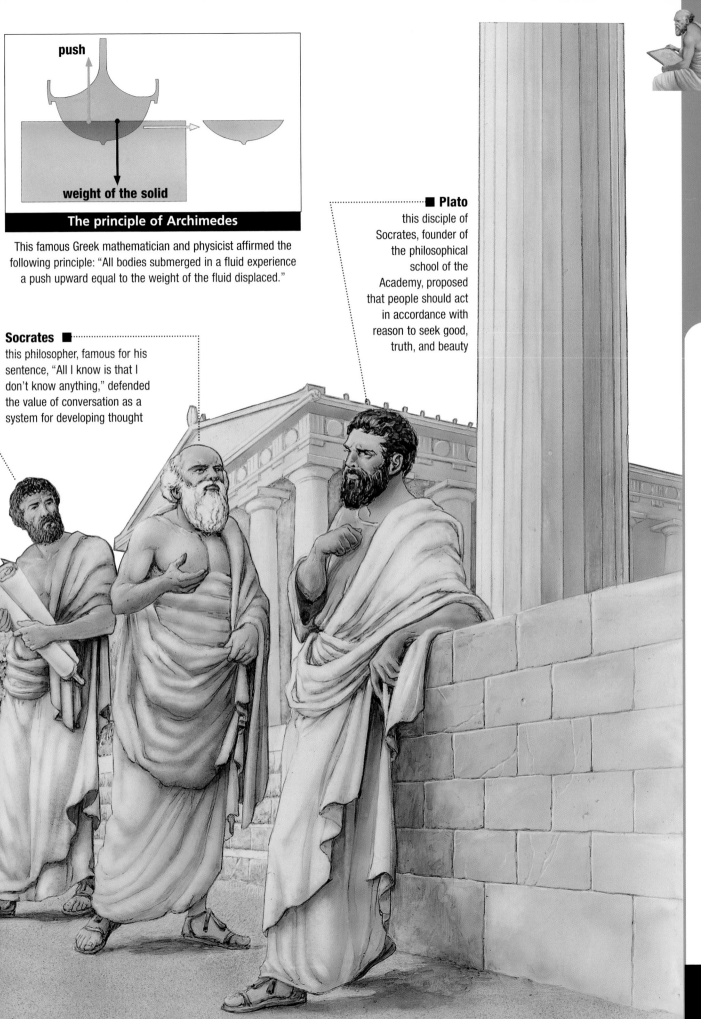

push

weight of the solid

The principle of Archimedes

This famous Greek mathematician and physicist affirmed the following principle: "All bodies submerged in a fluid experience a push upward equal to the weight of the fluid displaced."

■ Plato
this disciple of Socrates, founder of the philosophical school of the Academy, proposed that people should act in accordance with reason to seek good, truth, and beauty

Socrates ■
this philosopher, famous for his sentence, "All I know is that I don't know anything," defended the value of conversation as a system for developing thought

FIRST, THERE WAS CHAOS

At the beginning of time chaos ruled. And out of chaos emerged the older generation of gods, known as the Titans, whose leader, Kronos, was the god of time. From his union with Rhea, many children were born, but they were devoured by their father after birth. Their mother, however, managed to save Zeus, Poseidon, Hades, Demeter, and Hera from his voracity. Zeus confronted his father and beat him, becoming the god of the universe, the god with the most power.

THE MYSTERIES OF ELEUSIS

In the Hall of the Mysteries of Eleusis, or the Telesterion, near Athens, the Greeks celebrated formed secret cults to try to gain immortality. Little is known about these initiation rites; however, the characteristics of the building indicate that light played an important role.

■ **Mount Olympus**
the highest mountain in Greece; the ancient Greeks believed that the gods, ruled by Zeus, lived on its summit

■ **anthropomorphism**
Hellenic religion was also anthropomorphic; human forms were attributed to the gods

Poseidon ■
god of the sea and brother of Zeus; his principal attribute was the trident and he was usually depicted as an old man

Athena ■
goddess of wisdom; she was born from the head of Zeus; her most typical attributes are a lance, a shield, and a helmet crowned with a tuft of feathers

Artemis ■
goddess of the hunt and patron of women; she was the sister of Apollo; she is easily recognized because she usually carries a bow and wears sandals

Zeus ■
the most powerful Greek deity, ruling over the other gods; as a general rule, he is depicted seated on a throne with a lightning bolt in one hand and a scepter in the other

The oracle of the gods

A religious ceremony with the objective of divining the future through questions and offerings made to the gods through their mortal interpreters, priests and pythias (female fortunetellers). The most prestigious oracles were Apollo at Delphi (in drawing above, ruins of the temple), and Zeus in Dodona.

■ **heroes**
mortal beings, although some descended from the gods; their deeds and epic stories were the subject of legends

■ **polytheism**
the religion of ancient Greece was polytheistic because the Greeks believed in the existence of many gods

Aphrodite ■
goddess of beauty, love, and fertility; according to one tradition, she was born from sea foam, and was equipped with many charms

Apollo ■
god of the sun and the arts; could take the form of a clean-shaven youth with a lyre in his hand, or could appear in a chariot pulled by four horses and crowned in sunlight

Dionysus ■
god of wine and fertility; he usually takes the form of a clean-shaven youth, crowned with ivy or grape leaves, carrying in one hand a leafy stick, a cluster of grapes, or a cup

BETWEEN MYTH AND REALITY

Was it a legend, or did it really happen? In the *Iliad*, the famous epic poem, Homer narrates the battle of the Greeks against the Trojans, a story with the hero Achilles as the main character. Until archaeologist Heinrich Schliemann found the ruins of Troy, the historical authenticity of the events described could not be proven, but we now know that, at a time before Homer was born, there was an armed struggle between the Trojans and the Greeks. It ended with victory for the Greeks and the destruction of the city of Troy. The main protagonists of this legend follow.

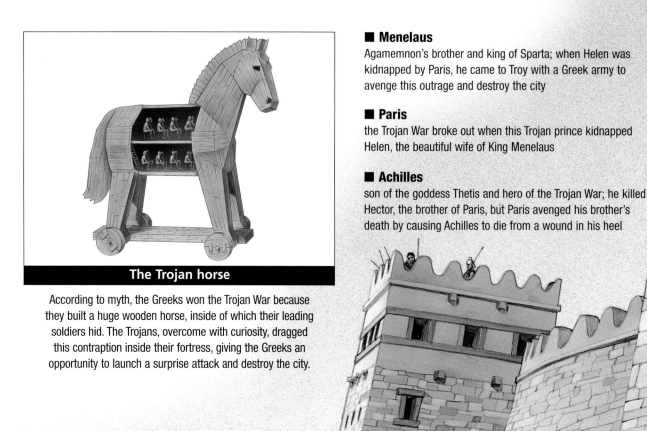

The Trojan horse

According to myth, the Greeks won the Trojan War because they built a huge wooden horse, inside of which their leading soldiers hid. The Trojans, overcome with curiosity, dragged this contraption inside their fortress, giving the Greeks an opportunity to launch a surprise attack and destroy the city.

■ **Menelaus**
Agamemnon's brother and king of Sparta; when Helen was kidnapped by Paris, he came to Troy with a Greek army to avenge this outrage and destroy the city

■ **Paris**
the Trojan War broke out when this Trojan prince kidnapped Helen, the beautiful wife of King Menelaus

■ **Achilles**
son of the goddess Thetis and hero of the Trojan War; he killed Hector, the brother of Paris, but Paris avenged his brother's death by causing Achilles to die from a wound in his heel

city gate ■

■ **defensive moat**

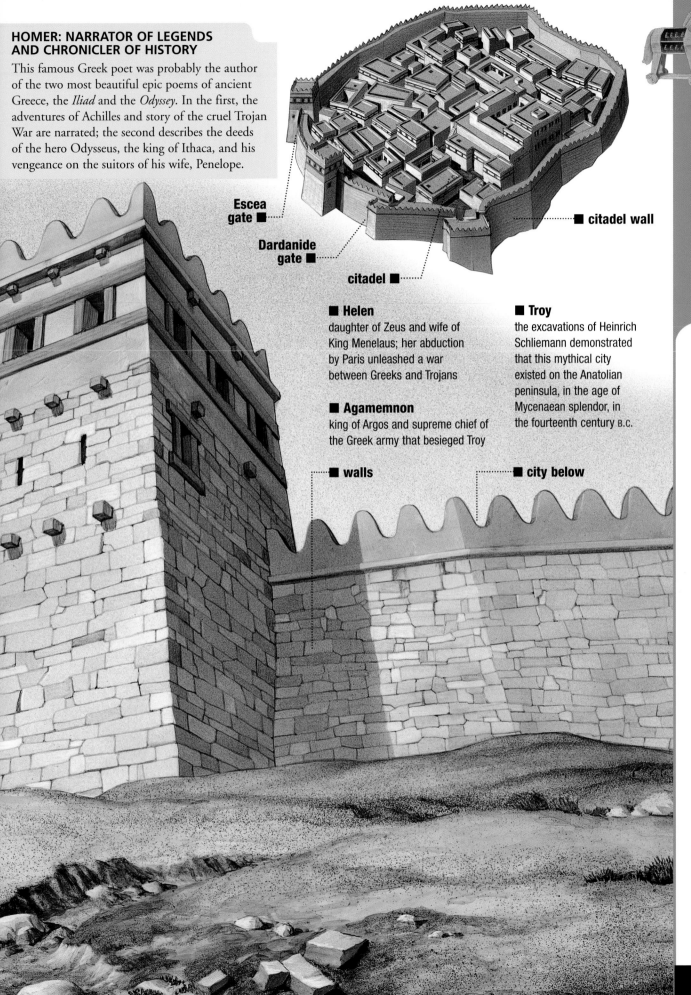

HOMER: NARRATOR OF LEGENDS AND CHRONICLER OF HISTORY

This famous Greek poet was probably the author of the two most beautiful epic poems of ancient Greece, the *Iliad* and the *Odyssey*. In the first, the adventures of Achilles and story of the cruel Trojan War are narrated; the second describes the deeds of the hero Odysseus, the king of Ithaca, and his vengeance on the suitors of his wife, Penelope.

Escea gate ■

Dardanide gate ■

citadel ■

■ citadel wall

■ **Helen**
daughter of Zeus and wife of King Menelaus; her abduction by Paris unleashed a war between Greeks and Trojans

■ **Agamemnon**
king of Argos and supreme chief of the Greek army that besieged Troy

■ **Troy**
the excavations of Heinrich Schliemann demonstrated that this mythical city existed on the Anatolian peninsula, in the age of Mycenaean splendor, in the fourteenth century B.C.

■ **walls**

■ **city below**

CLOSER TO THE GODS

At the highest point of the polis, often at the top of a hill, a sacred enclosure was reserved for the most important religious and civic buildings of the city. Inside this area, magnificent temples and theaters, adorned with splendid statues, were built. The acropolis of Athens, the most important and influential city-state of ancient Greece, was proof of the city's artistic, political, and cultural glory during the time when Pericles ruled.

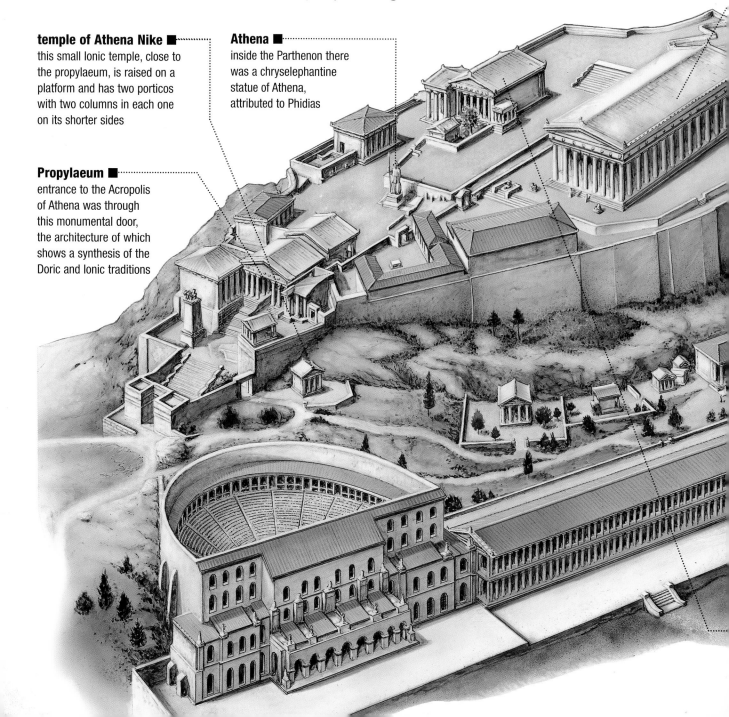

temple of Athena Nike ■
this small Ionic temple, close to the propylaeum, is raised on a platform and has two porticos with two columns in each one on its shorter sides

Athena ■
inside the Parthenon there was a chryselephantine statue of Athena, attributed to Phidias

Propylaeum ■
entrance to the Acropolis of Athena was through this monumental door, the architecture of which shows a synthesis of the Doric and Ionic traditions

■ Phidias

Greek painter and sculptor who supervised work on the Parthenon; in addition to the chryselephantine sculpture of Athena, also credited with the statue of Zeus for the temple of Olympus

■ Pan-Athenian festivals

festivals in honor of the goddess Athena; the pan-Athenian procession was brilliantly depicted in a relief sculpture that decorated the Parthenon

■ Parthenon

main temple of the acropolis of Athens, dedicated to the goddess Athena; was constructed in marble, according to the Doric and Ionic orders, and decorated with many sculptures

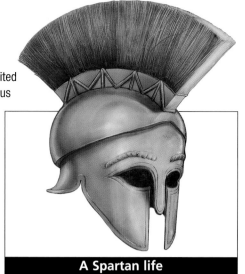

A Spartan life

Sparta was the second most important city-state in Greece, after Athens. The Spartans were subject to strict military discipline, fearing uprisings among those they colonized; from infancy, they were trained in the art of war, and domestic life was practically nonexistent, given the iron control that the state exercised over its citizens.

The Golden Age of Pericles

The political and cultural high point of Athens corresponds to the government of this famous strategist (443–429 B.C.), who ordered the reconstruction of the Athenian acropolis and surrounded himself with the most brilliant artists and intellectuals of the time.

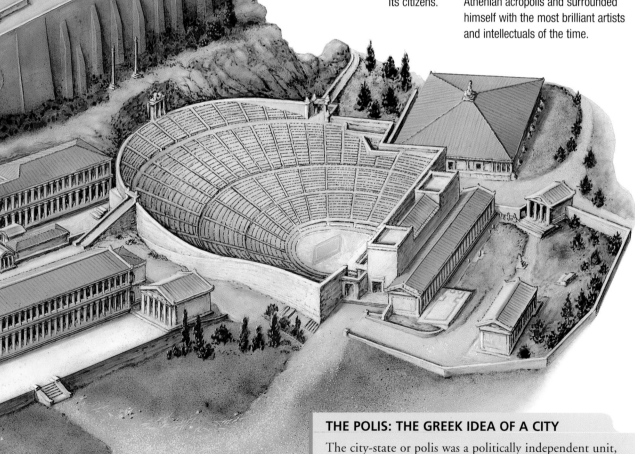

■ Erecteion

the most notable feature of this beautiful temple is the portico of the caryatids, statues of young women that hold up the roof

THE POLIS: THE GREEK IDEA OF A CITY

The city-state or polis was a politically independent unit, and after the introduction of democracy, the people participated in its organization and administration. The main public buildings, such as the *pritaneum* or city hall, were built around the agora, the nerve center of the city. The city-states also had farm and pasture lands, and were usually located near a port.

THE MEDITERRANEAN, A GREAT EMPIRE

Thanks to their naval ability, the Greeks were able to establish colonies at various spots on the Mediterranean coast, from the Black Sea to the far-away coasts of present-day Spain. Overpopulation, scarcity of land for cultivating, and internal struggles were the main reasons behind the voyages of exploration to discover new territories to settle or establish commercial relations. Navigation, commerce, and ceramics developed and flourished, and Greek culture was spread throughout the Mediterranean, while at the same time, it was enriched by new contributions from other cultures.

Massalia ■
name of the ancient Greek colony, the origin of present-day Marseilles, France

Ampurias ■
city founded by the Greeks in what is now Spain; archaeological excavations have uncovered the ruins of the ancient city

Iberian Peninsula

Greater Greece ■
this term refers to the group of colonies founded in the south of Italy and Sicily; the most important were Syracuse, Tarentum, Agrigentum, and Naples

Syracuse ■
city founded by the Greeks in Sicily; many buildings and monuments from this Hellenic period, such as the temple of Athena, still remain

trireme ■
typical ships of Hellenic war fleets; they had three orders of oars on the port side and the starboard side; estimated to have traveled at an average velocity of 9 kilometers per hour

Africa

Cyrene ■
main Greek colony in northern Africa, in what is now Libya

THALES OF MILETUS

Colonization brought with it a renewal and interchange of ideas and knowledge. In Miletus, the genius of Thales, a mathematician and philosopher of the Ionic school, stood out. He is credited with the first exact measurement of time with a sundial, a solar clock consisting of a vertical pole that projects a shadow on a flat horizontal surface.

Miletus ■
city in Asia Minor populated by
Greek colonizers; very important
cultural focal point whose
commercial expansion led to
the establishment of colonies on
the coasts of the Black Sea and
in Egypt

metropolis ■
the city of origin
of the colonizers

The drachma

The appearance of money favored
the economic and commercial
development of the Greeks. The
first coins began to be used toward
the end of the eighth century B.C.,
and spread rapidly around the
Mediterranean. The drachma was
the most widely-used monetary unit.

Euxine Sea ■
this is what the Greeks called the
Black Sea, on whose coast several
colonies dedicated mainly to
agriculture, such as Odessa and
Herakleia, were founded

an Peninsula

Anatolia

Mediterranean Sea

■ **Neukratis**
Egyptian city
founded by the
Greeks on the
Nile delta

Greek colonies ■
independent of the metropolis,
although they shared the
same religion and a similar
government structure

Nile River

THOSE CHOSEN BY THE GODS

You certainly have heard of the Olympic Games. The first Olympics were celebrated in the city of Olympus in the year 776 B.C. The ancient Hellenic people believed in discipline of the body and mind. This is why, every four years, they celebrated with athletic games featuring the best athletes of every specialty from all over Greece. This pan-Hellenic event, in honor of Zeus, the father of all the gods, was not limited to sports; it was also a festival of art and culture, and it attracted the most famous artists and intellectuals of the Hellenic world.

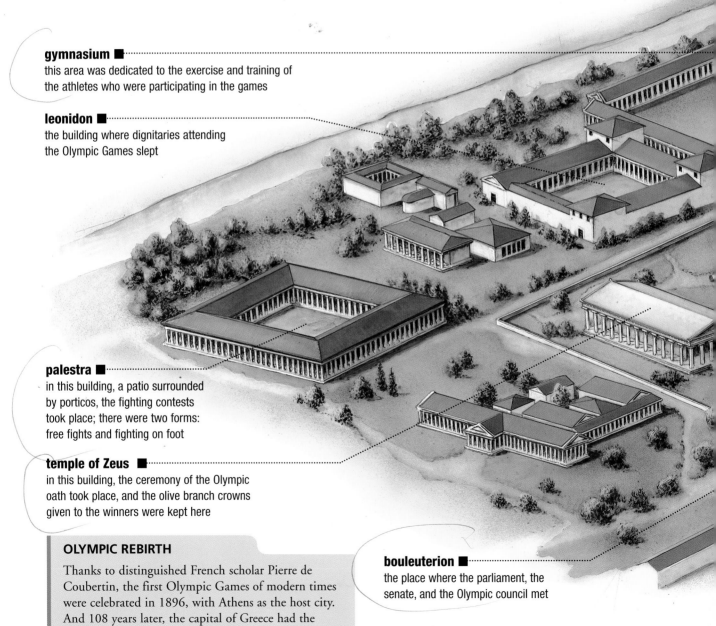

gymnasium ■
this area was dedicated to the exercise and training of the athletes who were participating in the games

leonidon ■
the building where dignitaries attending the Olympic Games slept

palestra ■
in this building, a patio surrounded by porticos, the fighting contests took place; there were two forms: free fights and fighting on foot

temple of Zeus ■
in this building, the ceremony of the Olympic oath took place, and the olive branch crowns given to the winners were kept here

bouleuterion ■
the place where the parliament, the senate, and the Olympic council met

OLYMPIC REBIRTH

Thanks to distinguished French scholar Pierre de Coubertin, the first Olympic Games of modern times were celebrated in 1896, with Athens as the host city. And 108 years later, the capital of Greece had the honor of repeating its role as host city.

THE MARATHON

Phidippides, a valiant Athenian athlete, ran 42 kilometers from Marathon to his city to bring news to the polis of the Greek triumph over the Persians at Marathon. He made the run so rapidly that he dropped dead after announcing the good news.

■ Olympic calendar

the games were celebrated in the spring and lasted five days; the first and last days were dedicated to ceremonies

■ winners

received a crown of olive branches and were greeted with great honors, such as the dedication of statues and poems written in their honor, upon their return to their homeland

The pentathlon

This was a trial divided into five parts: stadium running, discus throwing, javelin toss, long jump, and fighting. In each part, contenders were eliminated until there were only two athletes remaining, and these two battled for victory.

stadium ■

had a long track with two sharp curves and a finish line; in the longest straight areas there were steps. Different types of races were held there

■ hippodrome

this area was designated for horse racing; there were two types: chariot races and horse races

MATHEMATICS IN THE SERVICE OF ART

In the early stages of ancient Greek architecture, temples dedicated to the patron god of the city were built with wood and bricks, until these perishable materials were replaced by stone and later, marble. From a structural point of view, the house of the gods was conceived in proportion with human beings; the emergence of beauty and harmony through the mathematical perfection of forms and measures became the primary obsession of Greek craftsmen.

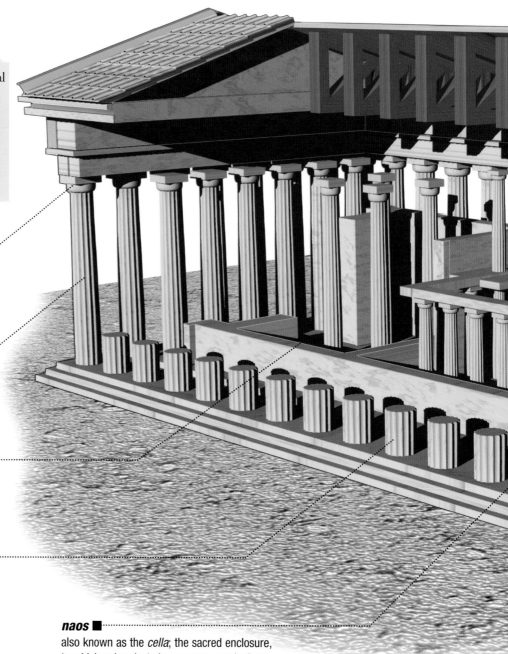

WORSHIP OF THE GODS

Consisted of offerings and animal sacrifices, complemented by prayers and hymns accompanied by musical instruments. Offerings were usually food and objects, and lambs were most frequently sacrificed.

capital ■
upper part of the column on which the entablature rests; Doric capitals are very simple; Ionic and Corinthian capitals, on the other hand, feature more complicated forms

shaft ■
part of the column between the base and the capital; it may be smooth, striated, or channeled

opistodomos ■
back part of the temple, opposite the *pronaos*, which has no communication with the *naos*

peristyle ■
colonnaded exterior or *periptera* of the temple; it surrounds the entire perimeter of the building

naos ■
also known as the *cella*; the sacred enclosure, to which only priests have access, and where the statue of the deity is erected

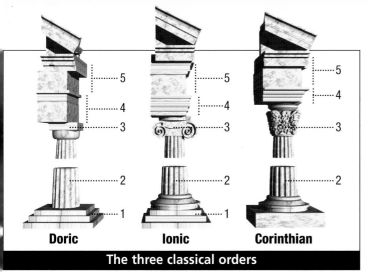

Doric   **Ionic**   **Corinthian**

1 stylobate
2 shaft
3 capital
4 architrave
5 frieze

The three classical orders

The Doric, Ionic, and Corinthian styles have distinctive features, above all in three architectonic elements: the frieze, the column, and the entablature.

THE DECORATION OF TEMPLES

Centered in the top part of the facade, in the main wall, and in the frieze. The capitals, particularly those of the Doric and Corinthian styles, were usually adorned with volutes, and in the case of Corinthian columns, with acanthus leaves.

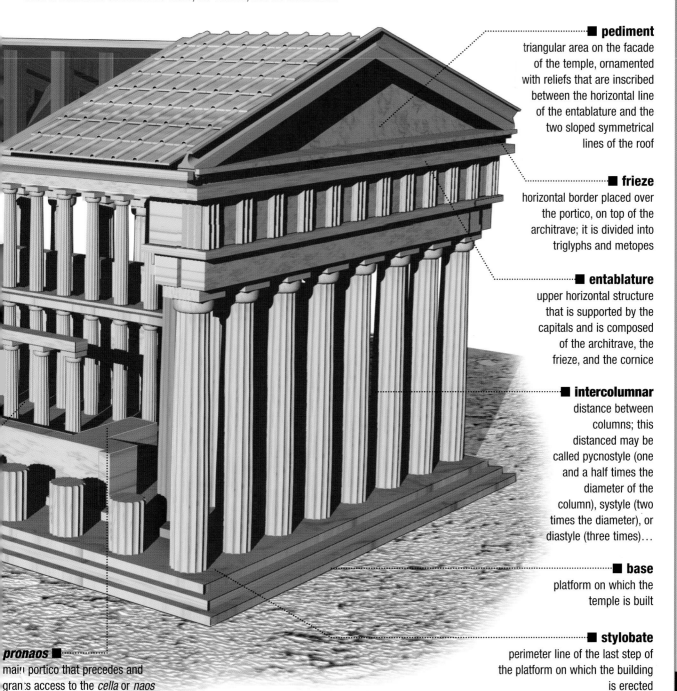

■ **pediment**
triangular area on the facade of the temple, ornamented with reliefs that are inscribed between the horizontal line of the entablature and the two sloped symmetrical lines of the roof

■ **frieze**
horizontal border placed over the portico, on top of the architrave; it is divided into triglyphs and metopes

■ **entablature**
upper horizontal structure that is supported by the capitals and is composed of the architrave, the frieze, and the cornice

■ **intercolumnar**
distance between columns; this distanced may be called pycnostyle (one and a half times the diameter of the column), systyle (two times the diameter), or diastyle (three times)…

■ **base**
platform on which the temple is built

■ **stylobate**
perimeter line of the last step of the platform on which the building is erected

pronaos ■
main portico that precedes and grants access to the *cella* or *naos*

FROM DRAMA TO COMEDY

In the cradle of Greek civilization, the joyous and jubilant celebrations in honor of Dionysus, the son of Zeus and god of wine and fertility, were transformed over time into scenes depicted in theaters before a public eager for distraction and diversion. There were two types of theatrical performance: tragedies and comedies. These performances took place in theaters, architectural spaces consisting of three parts: the *theatron*, the orchestra, and the *skene*.

TRAGEDY AND COMEDY

Aeschylus, the father of tragedy, brought a new character into the scene, an actor who engaged in a dialogue with the gods, creating the tragic form of drama. The celebrations that took place during the harvest gave way to comedy. Aristophanes was one of the most important masters of this form.

scenery ■
from the stands, normally made out of rock, one could usually take in the extraordinary panorama, forming an integral part of the theater and the scene

proscenium (*proskenion*) ■
balcony in the front part of the skene or construction that provided a background for the theater; where the actors were positioned

scene (*skene*) ■
the wide platform behind the orchestra where the dialogues between the characters who played the drama developed

orchestra ■
a circular space reserved for the movements of the chorus; in its center was the altar of Dionysus

public ■
sat in the stands, and would get involved in the action by reprimanding the actors

stands (*theatron*) ■
a graduated circular area where the public was seated; some curved aisles divided it into different sections and a concentric passageway separated it from the orchestra

■ tragedy

dramatic work in which the protagonist is generally guided toward catastrophe by passion or fate

■ comedy

critical, moralizing, or satirical drama with a happy ending

Dionysus was the god of fertility and the harvest. In the spring and summer a festival was held in his honor. His image was paraded around the city, followed by young people who represented satyrs, his companions. Before the altar of the god, they performed a chant called the dithyramb. A man whose face was covered by a mask portrayed the god and held a dialogue with the satyrs.

The festival of Dionysus

■ masks

actors and members of the chorus covered their faces with grotesque masks

THE PERFECTION OF FORMS

The ancient Greeks excelled in the art of sculpture and in painting. Unfortunately, few originals of their statues survive; most of those known today are Roman copies. However, we do have many samples of the reliefs that originally decorated the friezes and the front walls of temples and other buildings. The same is true of Greek monumental painting, lost almost completely; nevertheless, thanks to the diligent work of archaeologists, today we can still enjoy abundant ceramic art, whose pictorial decorations show an extraordinary mastery.

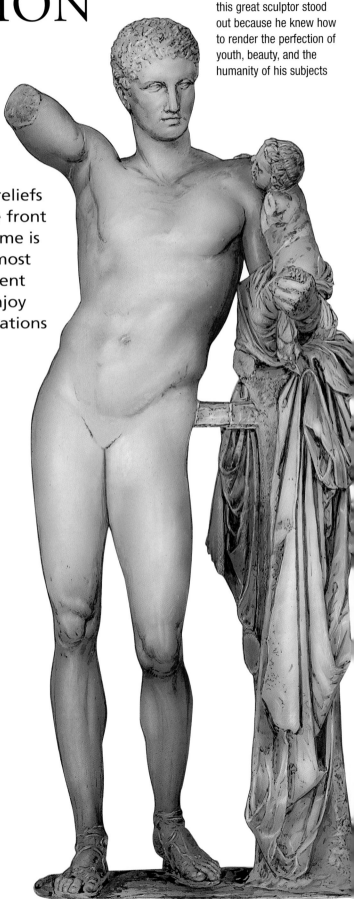

■ Praxiteles
this great sculptor stood out because he knew how to render the perfection of youth, beauty, and the humanity of his subjects

THE HUMAN BODY

Was given extraordinary importance and was brilliantly represented. The evolution from the first examples of the Archaic period, in which the figure lacks a sense of movement and maintains a certain hieratic quality, to the works of Hellenistic times, when the representation of movement and expression reached its highest point, is apparent.

■ themes
Greek sculpture had an eminently religious and commemorative nature; mythology and themes taken from everyday life, such as the depiction of young athletes, the struggles of warriors, or women with children, were the most common themes

■ materials
the most commonly used material was stone (limestone and marble), especially in reliefs, but in free sculpture, bronze, terracotta, and wood were also used, and, for chryselephantine statues, gold and ivory, were used

■ decoration
sculptures in stone were usually painted, and colored stones, glass, or ivory were used for the eyes

■ tools
the main instruments used by sculptors were various other types of chisels

■ scenes

the ornamental development of ceramic surfaces included scenes organized in parallel horizontal strips

evolution of pictorial forms ■

in the beginning very simple geometric forms were depicted, but with the passage of time these developed by adding the dimension of volume, and were embellished with representations of plants, animals, and finally, human beings

themes ■

predominantly mythological scenes; but there were also depictions of athletic competitions or military events and scenes from daily life

■ use

the uses for these pieces of pottery varied according to their shape. They could be used to store food and beverages or to carry out ritual sacrifices…

■ artists

there were two artists for a piece of pottery: the potter and the painter; pieces such as this were often signed by both

The canon of Polycleitos

The canon was a system of ideal proportions and relationships among the parts of a whole. In Polycleitos's system, the unit was the finger, and the total height of a body was seven times the size of the head.

■ amphora
large pot with two handles that was used primarily to store food and drinks

■ hydria
container with three handles used to hold water

■ *lekythos*
stylized urn with one handle

■ krater
very large pot used to mix water and wine

■ *pelike*
pot similar to an amphora, but with a wider base and not as tall

■ *pithos*
large wide pot that was used to store oil or grain

THE GREATEST OF THE CONQUERORS

The most outstanding of the Greek conquerors was Alexander the Great, the son of Phillip II, king of Macedon. He conquered Persia and led his armies as far as Egypt and India to form one of the greatest empires in the history of civilization. After his death, the lack of an heir to his vast empire led to the division of his territories, which were shared among his generals, and to the decline, and ultimately the disappearance, of Greek power.

■ **education**
the education of young Alexander was supervised by Aristotle, one of the greatest philosophers of all time

■ **Phillip II**
the king of Macedon and father of Alexander; he was assassinated by Pausanias

■ **Gordion knot**
an oracle promised the domination of Asia to the person who could undo a knot that tied the yoke to the steering pole of the cart consecrated to Zeus; Alexander cut the knot with his sword and was celebrated as a hero

■ **Alexandria**
Egyptian city founded by Alexander; with the creation of its legendary library, it became the most important cultural center of the classical East

■ Ptolemaic dynasty
this Macedonian dynasty governed in Egypt upon the death of Alexander the Great

■ Seleucid dynasty
one of the most powerful dynasties of the Hellenistic world, ruling over Syria and the territories of the empire of Alexander the Great

■ Kassander dynasty
of the three kingdoms that were formed after the death of the Conqueror, the Macedonian kingdom was governed by this dynasty

■ Hellenistic culture
during this period, Greek civilization reached its high point, marked by baroque refinements and sumptuousness of forms, freedom of artistic style, and complexity of spaces

The Laocoon

This group of sculptures, the most complete work of the period, shows the three main characteristics of sculpture at this time: baroque style, expressivity, and movement.

AN INVINCIBLE COMBAT FORMATION

Why were the armies of Alexander unbeatable on the battlefield? Because of the phalanx, a combat formation of the Greek infantry composed of sixteen rows of soldiers armed with lances that the intrepid Macedonian made lighter and more mobile by reducing the number of rows to eight.

■ Roxana
wife of Alexander and mother of his son, both assassinated by Kassander

GLOSSARY

Acanthus
Plant whose large lobed leaves were reproduced as an ornamental motif in Corinthian capitals.

Anthropomorphic
Displaying human or semi-human physical characteristics. The Greek gods were anthropomorphic.

Aristocracy
Form of government in which power is centered in the hands of the nobles or higher classes of society.

Bouleuterion
Building used for meetings of the Boule, a representative assembly of citizens that played a role in the government of the city.

Canon
Set of norms that regulate proportion and symmetry in art. These norms allow the establishment of harmony between each one of the parts of a work and the totality of the works, based on a certain range, in accordance with an ideal of beauty.

Caryatid
Sculpted female figure that replaces a column as a supporting element.

Cryselephantine
Scupture made of gold and ivory.

Cyclopean
A construction element of huge proportions. The walls of Mycenaean fortresses were Cyclopean because they were made of big blocks of stone.

Hellenic
Term referring to the Greeks, from the Greek work for their land, "Hellas." This term can be used to refer to the Greek mainland, the islands, and the Greek colonies.

Lintel
Beam placed in the upper part of an opening to support the weight of a wall built on top of it.

Mythology
Set of fabulous stories about the heroes and gods of antiquity.

Oligarchy
Form of government in which power is concentrated in the hands of a few.

Order
In architecture, set of elements used in the façade of a building. In ancient Greece, there were three architectural orders: Doric, Ionic, and Corinthian.

Pan-Hellenic
Term that refers to the union of the various regions of Greece.

Pythia
Priestess of Apollo who provided oracles in the sanctuary of Delphi.

Relief
Sculpture that sticks out from a flat surface.

Sphinx
Mythical character with the head of a woman, a winged body, and the limbs of a lion.

Stoa
Portico that was constructed in the agora of the Greek city-states to protect the citizens from the rays of the sun and inclement weather.

Strategist
In Greek antiquity, the head of an army. Starting with Cleisthenes, the concept was broadened to include ten members of a committee charged with the supervision of military and diplomatic affairs.

CHRONOLOGY

2000 B.C.	Minoan civilization.
1800 B.C.	First settlements in Troy.
1600 B.C.	Hegemony of Knossos. Tarentum and Mycenaean fortresses.
1300 B.C.	Trojan War. Fall of Knossos.
1100 B.C.	Fall of Mycenae. Beginning of the Dark Age.
1000 B.C.	First Greek colonies in Ionia.
800 B.C.	Growth of population in Greece. Main period of colonization. Appearance of alphabet system borrowed from the Phoenicians. First stone temple.
776 B.C.	First Olympic Games. First remains in the sanctuary of Olympus.
753 B.C.	Foundation of Rome. Epoch of the Homeric poems.
600 B.C.	The Assyrians arrive as far as the Mediterranean.
730–650 B.C.	Political power of the city-state. Sparta dominates the Peloponnese. Beginnings of Greek democracy. Beginning of the Archaic period. First temples walls decorated with sculptures. Archaic Doric period. First colossal temples in Ionia. Black figure pottery. First Greek coins.
600 B.C.	Beginning of the Peloponnesian Wars against Persia. Athens controls the Delphic league. Age of Pericles. Beginning of the Classical period. Temple of Zeus at Olympus. Parthenon and the reorganization of the Acropolis at Athens. Beginning of Greek urbanism. Red figure pottery. Beginning of theater; tragedy and comedy.
490 B.C.	Battle of Marathon.
400 B.C.	Reign of Alexander the Great. Maximum territorial expansion of Greece. Death of Socrates. Plato. Aristotle. Praxiteles. First manifestation of the Corinthian order: Tholos (circular temples).
323 B.C.	Death of Alexander the Great. Beginning of the Hellenistic period. Great Theater of Epidaurus.
300 B.C.	Library of Alexandria.
200 B.C.	Macedonian Wars. Beginning of Roman power. Great Altar of Zeus at Pergamon. *Venus de Milo. Winged Victory at Samothrace.*

INDEX